ROCKS ALL AROUND US

Mrs. Notowitz

By ANNE TERRY WHITE

Illustrated by EVELYN URBANOWICH

SCHOLASTIC  BOOK SERVICES

Published by Scholastic Book Services, a division of Scholastic Magazines, New York, N. Y

Grateful acknowledgment is made to Agnes Creagh, of the Geological Society of America, for her helpful suggestions about this book.

Rock collection on cover loaned through the courtesy of Claude M. Owen III; cover designed and photographed by Mike and Sonja Gilligan.

2nd printing . . . . March 1962
Manufactured in the U.S.A.

Contents

1. The Most Valuable Thing in the World

"I wonder what kind of rock this is!"

You may have said this many times. Stooping, you picked up a stone and turned it over in your hand. "Where did it come from?" you thought. "How was it made? Out of what?"

You may be sure that bit of rock had a story to tell. For every rock in the world has had adventures. Probably you tossed it away as a thing of no value. And you were right: rock is the commonest thing there is.

Yet it is the most valuable, too.

Every piece of rock has a story to tell.

Perhaps you think that air and water are more valuable. We couldn't live without them.

Yes. But much of our air and water came out of the rocks. And what is soil? Soil is crumbled rock with bits of dead plants in it. Without rock there could be no trees or grass. There could be no grain, no vegetables or fruit, no animals and no people.

Think how we depend on rocks! Look at the buildings made of stone. See the piers and bridges. A gravel driveway is rock. The glass in your windows comes from rock. Bricks and cement and plaster go back to rock. The dishes on your table were once rock. Coal is a rock. Oil comes out of rocks.

And metals. There's your bicycle. There are the cars, trucks, buses, trains, planes. All these come out of rock. So do rails and telephone wires. So do tools. And you can add lots more.

Under the fields is our ball of rock.

We live on a ball of rock. We forget that because so much of it is out of sight. It is covered with water, with soil, grass, and forest. But under all this is rock. The deepest ocean is just a scratch on top. Under it lie thousands of miles of rock.

2. The First Rocks

Long ago the ball of rock on which we live was very hot. It was so hot that all the rock was melted. And for millions of years it stayed that way.

Then, little by little, the outside of the ball cooled off. A thin crust formed. It was stiff and solid. In some places it was wrinkled. Those wrinkles were the first mountains.

There were cracks in the crust. Steam and air shot out of the cracks. The steam made thick clouds that hung all around the earth. The clouds wouldn't let the sun through even for a minute.

Then it began to rain. Never has there been such a rainstorm since. It rained and it rained, day and night, without letup. It rained for years. It rained for centuries. For the earth was still sizzling hot. As soon as the rain touched the earth, the water turned to steam. The steam would go up in clouds and come right down again as rain.

For countless years, rain fell without stopping.

Low places in the earth became seas and lakes.

By and by the outside of our rock ball really cooled off. It got so cool that the rain stopped turning into steam. Between rains the sun came out. The rain water ran off the rocks. It flowed into the low places of the earth's rock crust. Those low places became seas and lakes.

The lowest place of all was what we now call the Pacific Ocean. For there was an old, very deep scar here. It had formed before the rock crust had got quite stiff. A great mass of soft rock had flown off from this spot and shot up into space. It had become the moon.

Everybody knows where the Pacific Ocean lies. But where are those first mountains?

3. The Rocks Come Down

Many people have looked for traces of those early mountains. They have never found any. Those first mountains are all gone. Sun and rain and frost and air and wind and streams wore them away.

For all these worked to tear the rocks down then as they work to tear them down now. The work goes on very, very slowly. Some of the changes are so slow that you cannot see them. You cannot see the mountains grow smaller. When you are eighty, they will look the same to you as they do now. But you may be sure they will not be the same. Nothing in nature stays the same even for two minutes. The wearing and the tearing go on all the time. They never stop.

And the proof of that is all around you. The proof is in the fallen rocks at the foot of the hill. It is in the pebbles of the brook. It is in the sand of the seashore.

But how does the change take place? How is rock torn down and broken up?

Perhaps you already know that some things get a little bit bigger when they are heated. That's the way it is with rock. In the daytime the sun heats the outside of the rock, and it gets a little bigger. You can't see this happen, but you can see the results. For when the rock cools off, it shrinks a little bit. And when it shrinks, it cracks.

Air gets into the cracks. It eats away the rock, widening the cracks.

Rain gets in. Up on the mountain it is cold at night. The water in the cracks freezes.

Now water doesn't act the same way as rock. Water gets a little bit bigger when it turns to ice. Then it has great power. You have seen it at work. You may have taken a bottle of milk — which is mostly water — into the house on a freezing day. The milk had pushed the cap right off and squeezed itself out of the bottle.

Well, the water in the cracks can't push up a cap and get out. But it must have room to freeze. So it pushes against the rock and cracks it. Big pieces and small pieces break off. The pieces of rock come tumbling down the mountain. If there is a road near by, people in cars have to be warned: "Look out for fallen rocks!"

Streams carry pebbles and sand to the sea.

Mountain streams run fast. In the spring they rush madly downhill. For then they are full of rain and melted snow. They pick up rocks that the sun and air and frost have broken off.

The rocks grind and scrape against the bed of the stream. They file it. They cut deeper and deeper into the rock. They wear it down. Sometimes stones get caught in an eddy. Then they swirl around and around. They scour out a great round hole in the bedrock. You may have gone swimming in such a hole. You may have caught fish in it.

The rocks in the stream grind and scrape against one another, too. Pieces get broken off. The smaller pieces break into still smaller ones. The rough edges become smooth. The chips break up into sand and clay. If you pick up a pebble from a brook, you can feel how smooth and round it is on all sides. It has no sharp edges at all.

Perhaps you have picked up a stone like that. If you did, those smooth edges told you a piece of its story right there. That stone had traveled a long way by water. All its roughness had been knocked off, and scraped off, and scoured off.

Where is the mountain stream going?

Most streams end in the sea. Big or small, fast or slow, they carry their load down to the river's mouth and dump it. In the spring the rivers dump huge loads of *sediment* in the sea. That is what we call the pebbles and sand and clay that rivers carry.

All along the edge of the sea something else has been hard at work. The waves have been battering the cliffs. The waves are never still.

They pick up sand and pebbles, and blast the rocks with them. They pound away. Hour after hour, day after day, they pound. After a while they wear a hollow at the base of the cliff. The upper part juts out like a shelf. As time goes on, there is less and less to hold up that shelf. Then along comes a storm. The wind blows up giant waves. They blast the shelf with sand and pebbles and rocks.

The shelf comes crashing down. It breaks

into a thousand pieces. The sandy surf thunders over the pieces. It scours the boulders and files them down. By and by there are no boulders left. There isn't even a pebble. All is sand.

Next time you are at the seashore and dig your toes into the sand, remember: all of this was once a cliff.

The sea pounds away at the edge of the land.

4. Patchwork Rocks

From cliff to boulder. From boulder to pebble. From pebble to sand. Every minute something is breaking. Every minute something is moving. The rocks are going into the sea.

But nature wastes nothing. What is taken away on one hand is given back on the other. There will be patching and piecing. Out of the bits torn down and broken up, nature will make new rocks. They will be patchwork rocks.

It takes a long time to make rock out of sediment. Year after year the stream dumps its load. Year after year it brings its gift of pebbles and sand and mud to the sea.

Sandstone often makes a library.

The waves play with the sediment. They pick up the pebbles and sand and mud, and sort and drop them. They drop the heaviest part first. That's the pebbles. They carry the sand a little farther out to sea. The light mud they carry out farthest.

But sometimes there is a storm. Then things get mixed up. For the storm waves are very strong. They sweep the pebbles out farther than before. They spread pebbles on top of sand. They spread sand on top of mud. There is a layer of this and a layer of that.

Hundreds of years pass. Thousands of years go by. And all the time the waves sort and spread, sort and spread: fine layer, coarse layer, fine layer, coarse layer.

By and by the layers are very thick and heavy. The top layers press hard on the bottom layer. It gets all squeezed down. Tiny grains get in between the bits. They cement everything together. Now down on the bottom you have rock. We call it *sedimentary* rock because it was made out of sediment.

Do you live in the middle of our country? Then most of the rock at your doorstep will be sedimentary. For a sea once covered this part of America, as it did many other parts, too. The water is gone now. But not the rock that was made on the floor of that sea. It was raised up millions of years ago. When you pass a place where a road or railway cuts through rock, stop and look. You will see the patchwork rocks lying in layers. They will look like a pile of books one on top of another.

Perhaps some stone you have picked up was a bit of patchwork rock. Perhaps it was made from the sand which a forgotten river brought down to that forgotten sea. If so, it would be called *sandstone*. Was it yellow, buff, brown, red, gray, or green? It doesn't matter. Sandstone is sandstone, no matter what color. The color comes mostly from the bits of cement. This is a good stone for building. Many a town library is built of sandstone. Many a courthouse is sandstone.

In the Middle West there are great beds of very pure sandstone that is too good to build with. Much of it is used for making the best glass. Quite likely the windows of your bank came from those beds. Perhaps someone you know has a pair of eyeglasses made of the St. Peter sandstone from Illinois and Missouri.

Shale may be used for brick, tiles, or cement.

Was your stone so fine that you couldn't pick out the individual grains? Then maybe it was *shale*. Shale is made out of the clay and mud the waves carried out to sea. Gray would have been the usual color. But shale may be pink or red, black, brown, buff, or green. If it was shale, then probably it was very soft. Most shales are. You might have cut it with a knife. Such shales are good only for making brick, tiles, and cement.

Or maybe your stone was *conglomerate* — made out of pebbles and sand cemented together. If the pebbles were smooth and rounded, you may be sure it was conglomerate. But if the little stones had sharp edges, then it was *breccia*.

Conglomerate and breccia contain bits of older rock.

Those sharp stones plainly told you their story. They had not traveled far. If they had, their sides would have been smooth.

Probably they fell into mud right where they were chipped off. Probably they stayed there till the mud turned to stone around them.

5. Lichen on a Rock

Most of the rock all around us is soil. How did it get there? How did it come to cover so much of the great rock ball on which we live?

Making soil is a slow, slow business. It took endless time for cold and heat and air and rain to tear down the bare rock and crumble it. After that, for thousands of years the air and water kept working on the crumbled rock. Little by little they took away some of the materials of which the rock was made. Other materials changed. And slowly the rock rotted. Chemicals were formed in it such as plants could use for food. Then at last a few growing things would take root. They died, mixed with the crumbled rock, and more plants grew on top.

Much of our soil was made this way. But much was not.

Perhaps somewhere out in the country you have seen a rock with a dull, gray-green look about it. It is not the true color of the rock. Bend close and look. You will see that tiny flat plants are growing there. When you pass your hand over it, crumbs of the rock roll off.

The tiny plants are lichens. They don't need soil to live on. They can get a hold on the bare rock. The lichens have poured their juices on it. Bit by bit they will soften and crumble the rock. When the lichens die, they will mix with the crumbs and with dead leaves and form a little soil.

Perhaps there is a crack in the rock where a lot of the crumbs and lichen have collected. Some plant is growing in it. It is a chokecherry tree springing up. The roots of the chokecherry will spread the crack. In the end they will split the rock. Bit by bit it will crumble. The dead

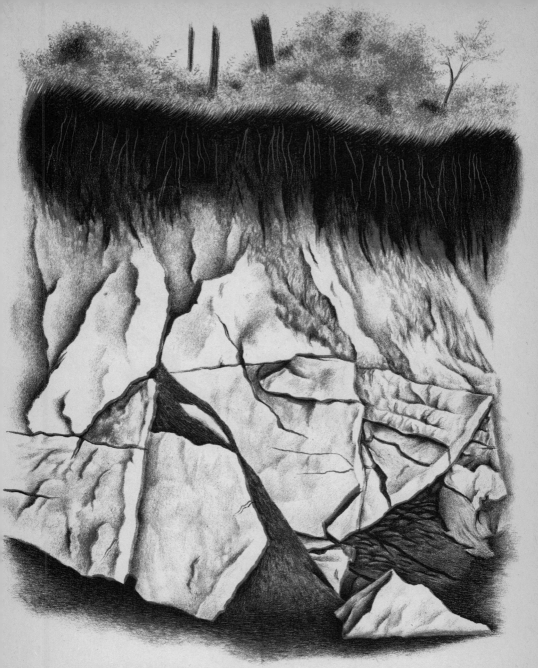

Crumbled rock and dead plants turn into soil.

Lichens make rock soft and crumbly.

leaves will mix with the crumbled rock and
lichen.

These are the ways in which nature has
worked for millions of years to make our soil.
It is not very deep. In most places the topsoil
goes down only a foot or two.

Is there a cellar being dug near you? Then you have a fine chance to see what lies under the soil. You will find a second layer under the first. It will be lighter in color because there are no dead plants in it. It is just crumbled, rotted rock. Under this lies bedrock. Bedrock is the unbroken rock crust.

6. Up from Below

What is that crust like? Do we measure it in feet or miles?

We don't know a great deal about the crust of our rock ball. We think it is only about fifty miles thick. But, of course, nobody has been down to see. The deepest mine is only two miles deep. The deepest hole we have ever dug is only four miles deep.

Yet we do know this. The crust gets hotter and hotter as we go down. Our deepest mines have to be air-cooled. Surely fifty miles under our feet it is hot enough to melt rock.

Is all the rest of our rock ball melted, then?

Bubbling hot rock bursts from the mouth of a volcano. It has risen from deep inside the earth.

Mount Hood is a volcano that may be only sleeping.

Strangely, no. Tests show that for about half way to the center of the earth the rock is rigid. Though it is hot enough to melt, it doesn't melt. For if it melts, it must get bigger. And there is no room for it to get bigger. It can't get out and spread. The miles and miles of rock above won't let it move.

Yet once in a while we get a hint of what's going on below. Somehow or other a little of the deep rock does melt. It eats its way through the rocks above. It finds a weak place in the crust. And with a roar of steam and gas it breaks out. Then we see what it is like down under the crust. For the *lava,* or melted rock, that comes pouring out of a volcano is bubbling hot.

You may not have heard that we have volcanoes in this country. But we do. Counting big ones and small ones, we have hundreds. Most of them are dead, to be sure. We don't expect lava to come gushing out of them any more. But Mount Lassen in California blew up in 1915. Mount Hood in Oregon and Mount Rainier in Washington are still warm in spots. We may see fireworks out of them yet.

For we can never be sure about a volcano. There is one in Italy that people thought was dead. But it was only sleeping. After a thousand years it woke up. The lava and gases that poured out of that volcano killed eighteen thousand people. The ash buried two cities.

It is scary to watch a volcano that is acting up. The earth shakes and rumbles. Clouds of steam pour out. Red-hot rocks and cinders shoot high. They curve out and fall back down, building a round hill about the opening. They build the hill higher and higher. Then melted rock gushes out. It flows down the hill, or cone as it is called. Sometimes it flows on for miles. Everything in the lava's path is lost.

This is one of the few things nature does fast. A few years ago a new volcano started up in a cornfield in Mexico. The very first day the cone grew 200 feet tall. In nine years it rose to 1,600 feet. It spread melted rock over a hundred square miles all around the cone. In many places that lava was 300 feet deep.

Melted rock, pouring out, builds up the volcano.

Basalt may be found in columns with six sides.

Have you sometimes broken open a stone?
Did it have a velvety look inside? Were the
grains so fine that you couldn't pick them out?
Then perhaps your stone was a piece of lava
rock. And most likely it was *basalt*. For basalt
is the commonest lava rock there is.

Most of our basalt didn't come out of
volcanoes. It poured out of great cracks in the
earth and spread like a blanket. Our biggest
stretch of basalt is in Washington, Oregon, and
Idaho. If you live in one of those states, you

have seen it a thousand times on the roads. Crushed basalt makes a fine hard-top for roads.

There are basalt quarries in New Jersey. There are some in the Connecticut Valley, too. The road often passes right through basalt. On either side you see a wall of rock. It is reddish-orange. For the air has changed the outside color. Inside it is dark gray or even black.

It is a thrill to pass a wall of basalt. For once this rock was boiling hot. It came pouring out of the earth.

You can be very sure of this. For you can see at once that this isn't sedimentary rock. There are no layers. No, this rock was not laid down by water. It came up fiery hot from far down under the crust of our rock ball.

There may be some lava rock closer to you than you think. For your dentist uses a *pumice* powder to clean your teeth. There may be pumice, too, in the scouring powder by your sink.

Pumice is one of the strangest rocks there is. It is a rock foam. It formed on top of lava

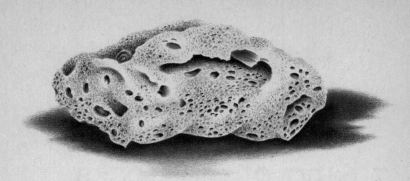

spurting out of a volcano just the way foam forms on top of boiling jam.

In olden days you would have found a piece of this odd rock in many a kitchen. Your great-grandmother scoured her pots with it. It was handy when you got ink on your fingers, too. Lying on the soap dish, the rock looked just like a sponge full of tiny holes. You were surprised when it didn't soften up in water.

Those holes had gas in them once, but it got out when the rock hardened. There are air pockets in pumice still. They make pumice so light that it will float. It is the lightest rock in the world.

7. King of the Rocks

There is another rock that comes up hot from below. It is *granite*. Some people call it king of the rocks because it is so strong. But it is more than just strong. You can cut it in almost any shape. And when you polish it, it shines. So it is one of the best rocks in the world.

Now here is the strange thing about granite: it comes up from far down, but it doesn't get all the way to the top. Sometimes granite finds room for itself between layers of rock and spreads out like a sheet. Sometimes it worms its way into up-and-down cracks in the rocks. Sometimes it pushes up into the insides of

Granite pushes up under the top layer of rock.

mountains. Once in a while it gets right through the layers of rock close to the top of the earth. There it arches up the layered rocks above it and spreads out like a mushroom. It stays like that. It stays and cools under the rock lid. We don't see the granite until the lid wears away.

Everybody has seen the king of the rocks. For there is a granite monument in nearly every town. But not everyone has held a piece of granite in his hand.

When you do, you see, at once that granite is a speckled rock. Some of the specks are light and some are dark. But all are about the same size. Some of the light ones look like sharp pieces of glass. Other light grains are smooth. You can peel off a few of the dark flakes with your nail. Other dark specks won't come off.

So you may think that there are four different kinds of things here.

Yes. They have been cooked together. But you can still tell them apart. In a fruit cake you can tell which are the nuts and which the raisins and other fruits. In granite you can tell the *minerals* apart. The light, glassy ones are *quartz*. The light ones with smooth sides are *feldspar*. The dark specks you can peel off are black *mica*. The other dark specks are *hornblende*.

Granite is a good rock for buildings.

Now all granite is grainy. That's how it gets its name. And all granite is made the same way. It is cooked down in the deep, dark kitchens of the earth. Yet the rock may be many colors. That's because the feldspar in it isn't always the same. Granite takes its color from the feldspar. So granite may be gray or pink, yellow, red, or green.

Have you ever seen granite with grains as big as peas?

They can be that size and even bigger. It depends on how long the granite took to cool. If it cooled quickly, the grains are small. If it cooled slowly, the grains are big. There is one kind of granite that has huge grains. It is called giant granite. A single piece of mica in giant granite has weighed 90 tons. One piece of feldspar filled two freight cars.

There is lots of granite in our country, both east and west. If you live in New England, granite is the rock you know best. You don't have to go to the mountains to find it, for granite boulders are all around you.

These boulders were a puzzle once. "How

A *glacier* dropped the *granite* rocks in this field.

did they get here?" people asked. "Did a flood bring them?"

We have the answer now. An ice cap, or glacier, once lay over large parts of our north. The glacier moved very slowly. It scraped over the mountains and rounded them. It carried along huge pieces of rock. It pushed great loads of rocks and earth in front of it. It acted like a giant snowplow.

A glacier scours the land.

The ice melted thousands of years ago and left behind the boulders it had torn from the mountains. The farmers have picked up the smaller rocks and piled them into walls. Others still lie in the fields. Some of the rocks are as big as houses. Some fields in New England are nothing but boulders, and many of them are granite.

In the Mississippi Valley you see almost no granite. But it is there. If you dug down, then drilled, you would come to granite at last. Under the soil, under the layered rocks, lies granite. The continents are mostly granite.

8. What the Sea Left Behind

There is a rock which you use every day of your life. It stands in the kitchen by the stove. It goes on the table three times a day.

It is *salt*.

There will never be a shortage of salt in America, for we have beds of rock salt hundreds of feet thick. They stretch for miles under the ground. In our salt mines tunnels are cut in solid salt. Tracks are laid right on salt.

Where did all this salty treasure come from?

It is a long story that begins back when the first rains fell on earth. Those first rains

Old seas left us great beds of rock salt.

began to dissolve salt out of the rocks. Rivers carried the salt down to the sea, and the sea became salty.

Of course the sea wasn't nearly as salty then as it is now. The sea is getting saltier all the time. For the rain keeps on dissolving salt out of the rocks. And the rivers keep on bringing it to the sea. Yet the amount of water in the sea stays about the same.

It stays the same because water is always

leaving the ocean. The sun shines on the ocean and heats it. Some of the water turns to vapor. The vapor turns to clouds. Then rain falls on the land again. It runs into the rivers which run into the sea. Over and over it's the same thing. There is no end to it.

But how did salt mines get to be in Kansas and Oklahoma? How did they get to Michigan and Texas and New York?

We can thank the old seas for that. Those old seas came and went. Every time the land sank, the water came in. Many times America looked like a lot of little islands. Then the land would rise again and the seas would roll back.

Now, once in a while the water didn't *all* go back. An arm of the sea was cut off and left behind in some low place. The water in that cut-off arm dried up. But the salt that had been in the water stayed.

In some places you can see the salt above the earth. Animals find it and lick it. They love their salt licks, and will travel miles to get to them. Animals have helped us discover where our hidden salt lies.

Those old seas gave us another useful rock. It is one your teacher uses every day, perhaps. You may use it, too, sometimes. Very likely your school has boxes and boxes of it. It can be many colors. But when it is pure, it is snow-white. It is the white kind that you use in school.

Chalk and blackboards both come from rock.

You call it *chalk*. But very little school chalk is really chalk. Most school chalk is *gypsum*.

We have huge beds of gypsum which the old seas left behind. Oklahoma has more than any other state. Sometimes it is called the gypsum state.

Gypsum is a rock so soft that you can scratch it with your nail. It is easy to grind into powder. And that's what happens to most of it. It is ground, then burned to drive the water out. That makes plaster of Paris.

Perhaps you once had a toy made out of gypsum. It may have been a little animal. It was the simplest thing in the world to make. Somebody just added water to plaster of Paris, then poured it into a mold. After a while the plaster "set." And there was your toy.

9. Rocks Out of Shells

It is spring. Everybody is out working on his lawn. Across the road a man is scattering something white on his grass. He is putting on *lime* to make the grass grow better.

You have seen lime used that way before, and perhaps in other ways too. When men make a new sidewalk, they mix in lime. When they build an asphalt road, they use lime. You may have seen the rock wool unloaded for a new house. Then men perhaps told you rock wool is made of lime. They were going to put it in the walls to keep the house warm in winter and cool in summer.

Limestone is a rock of many uses.

Lime is crushed limestone. You can always tell this rock by a very simple test. Just pour a little vinegar on it. If it fizzes, it is limestone.

We have beds of limestone all over America. And that's lucky, for we find more ways to use limestone than any other rock. We use it in cement. We use it in making paper and glass and soap. Many fine buildings are made of limestone. In some, large shining slabs of it make walls and floors. Still bigger slabs make bridges. Take a good look at the next bridge you come to. If it is white or cream-colored, the chances are it is limestone.

Now how was this rock made? Did it come up boiling hot from under the crust, or was it laid down by water?

Neither. Limestone is a very strange rock. Nearly all of it was made by plants and animals of the sea. They made it out of lime.

How did lime get into the sea in the first place?

It got there in the same way that salt did. Water dissolved it out of the rocks. And most of the job was done by water under the ground.

For the rain that sinks into the earth is not lost. It travels down and down. Taking its time, it drips through tiny pores in the rock. And as it drips, it dissolves. It does a good job because it isn't in a rush. Sometimes the water gets very far down in the bedrock. But in the end it has to turn aside. For it gets to rock that is too hard, and it can't get through. Then it just rolls along on its hard rock bed till at last it gets into the sea.

If you dip up a cup of sea water, you won't be able to see the lime in it. But there are plants and animals that have the power to use what we cannot see. Every little sea shell you have ever picked up was made of lime.

And now you see where a great deal of our limestone comes from. Millions and millions of shelled creatures lived and died in the sea. When they died, their shells fell to the bottom. The shells piled up and piled up. Broken and crumbled bits of shell filled the places in between the shells. Then everything was pressed so hard that it turned to rock.

We have limestone on top of some of our mountains. We can see the very shells in the rock. It is a shock to come upon them, for they speak to us of something we didn't expect. They clearly tell us that these mountains were once the bottom of a sea.

Sea creatures make their shells of lime.

There are many kinds of shell limestone. Some are made of whole shells. Some are made of crushed shells. There is one kind made out of bits of coral. Another is made from what was left of little animals something like our starfish.

But the shell limestone we know best is *chalk — real* chalk.

You would never guess that real chalk is made of shells. It looks just like white powder pressed together. The shells are so tiny you can't see them. But put a bit of real chalk under a glass that makes things many times bigger; you will see the shells then. In a stick of real chalk there are millions and millions of tiny shells.

Shells pressed together make limestone.

The animals that once filled these shells lived on the top of the sea. They died, and their shells drifted to the bottom. Day and night they fell. No eyes could see that strange white rain. But it went on and on. The shells kept falling and falling for millions of years. They made beds thousands of feet thick. Now those tiny shells are rock.

The White Cliffs of Dover are on the coast of England across from France. Those white cliffs are chalk. They are some of the last bits left of a great chalk bed. The English Channel runs there now. Long ago the water cut its way through the chalk, turning England into an island. Before that, people could walk from France to England. And that's how cave men got to England. They walked across the chalk from France.

We have chalk beds in Kansas and Texas. But though chalk is such a pretty rock, it is too soft for building. Most of it is burned for lime. Some goes into tooth powder. Some gets into paint. And some finds its way to school.

Tiny shells form the White Cliffs of Dover.

10. Rocks That Have Changed

Take a good look at the blackboard in school. For the blackboard, too, is rock. It is a rock that has changed.

All rocks change, of course. We know how they are worn away. We know how, little by little, new rocks are made out of the broken bits. But some rocks change *before* they are worn away. Like people, they have changed because they have been through so much.

To be sure, all rocks have to stand a great deal. The wind blasts them. The rain washes and dissolves them. The waves batter them. The air eats at them. The sun heats them. The

*The Indians
knew how
to make heat
by rubbing.*

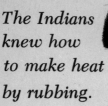

frost and ice crack them. But some rocks have to bear much more: they have to endure great heat. And that changes them.

We would guess it because we know what happens to clay in a kiln. Our cups and plates and teapots were once common clay. The clay was shaped into dishes. And the dishes were put in a kiln to bake. They came out changed. They went in soft and dull, and came out firm and hard and glassy.

Now rocks don't pass through a furnace, but some of them have to lie next to granite. And when granite comes up from below, it is much hotter than a roaring furnace. So the rocks around the granite get baked. Hot water and steam change rocks, too. But most of them get hot by rubbing and pressing.

The Indians knew that rubbing and pressing made heat. They would rub two sticks together till they got a spark. We know, too. On a cold day we rub our hands together to get them warm.

This is just what happens to rocks. Where they rub and grind together, they get hot. Where they break and slide past each other, they get hot. Where rocks are bent and folded, they get hot. Then a great change takes place. The minerals in the rocks shift around. They sort themselves out. The light specks get together, and the dark specks get together. So the rock looks striped. The rock called *gneiss* is usually like that.

Now, any rock can change. Even coal can change. The harder it is pressed, the harder the coal becomes. We have coal that has become so hard it will hardly burn. It has changed into *graphite*. Luckily we can use it for something else. The "lead" in your pencil is graphite.

Very often rocks change for the worse. There's granite. It is the king of rocks. But when granite changes to granite gneiss, it is spoiled for many things. It splits too easily. Sandstone, too, is often worse when it changes. It becomes *quartzite*, and quartzite may be full of cracks.

But some rocks change for the better. The rock that makes your blackboard is an example. Once it was shale. It wasn't of much use. It changed to *slate* and is now very useful.

Is your roof made of slate? Then perhaps there is an extra piece around. Set it in a wooden frame and you will have just such a slate as every schoolboy and girl once had. Paper used to cost a lot. It was much cheaper to wash a slate clean and start fresh.

Slate is useful for black boards and roofing.

Marble is another rock that has changed for the better. Once it was crumbly shell limestone. Now it is the queen of rocks. It can be many colors, for marble gets its color from the kind of shells that made the limestone. It can also be marbled. That is, it can be splotched with color. All kinds are wanted, all kinds are quarried. But pure white marble is wanted most of all. That's because it won't split when it is carved and will take a high polish. The proudest statues are made of marble.

Marble goes into statues and buildings.

11. Rocks That Were Once Alive

A heavy truck backs up to the cellar window. The driver sets up a chute, and a stream of black, shiny *coal* starts sliding into the bin.

What are these black stones? Why can they burn and give out heat when other stones cannot?

Coal has the power to warm us because once it was alive. Ages ago it was trees and ferns and other plants that died and turned to rock.

Sometimes dead plants mix with crumbled rock and make oil. But not always. When plants grow in a swamp, something else may

Coal gives off heat stored millions of years ago.

happen. In our country it happened on a very large scale. That's why we have so much coal.

It happened when the old seas were going away. Much of our land was still under water then. But in some places there was swamp, not sea. The climate was warm and damp the way it is in a hothouse. And just as in a hothouse, plants shot up overnight.

Great forests grew in the swamps. There were tall ferns with fronds five and six feet long. Rushes grew to thirty feet. Trees a hundred feet high towered over them. Some

Plants of ancient forests have turned to coal.

Great insects lived in the swampy forests.

were the great-great-grandparents of our pines. But instead of needles they had leaves like blades. Instead of cones they had long bunches of seeds.

Strange insects lived in those strange forests. Four-inch roaches crept among the roots. Huge dragonflies shot to and fro. With their wings spread out, they were almost a yard across.

The trees and ferns and rushes drank in the sunshine. They turned it into food for themselves, storing it in their cells as starch. And year by year they dropped their leaves and seeds and stems into the swamp. The bog took in everything. The layer of dead plants grew thicker and thicker. And always new plants grew on top.

Then slowly the swamp and the land around began to sink. Water ran into the bog, for water must run downhill. It covered the dead plant layer. It covered the growing forest. Streams dumped sediment on top. And the sediment turned to rock.

Down under it the black muck had already become peat. Now the peat was getting pressed harder and harder. At last it turned to coal.

The lumps going down the chute are that stored sunshine of long ago. When we burn coal, we get back the heat those old trees and ferns and rushes took from the sun. The coal itself tells us the story. For the leaves, the stems, the seeds of that great swamp forest can all be seen in the coal. Even the giant roaches are there. Even the dragonflies with their monster wings are there.

12. From Seaweeds and Algae

"Fill 'er up!"

The gas station man unscrews the cap and sticks a nozzle in the tank. A smell of gasoline floats on the air. You get out of the car to watch how many gallons the tank will take.

Cars whiz by on the highway. Red ones, blue ones, tan ones, green, yellow, pink.

Every one of them will have to pull up at a filling station. They will all have to stop for gas some place. Where does all that gas come from? And what is this stuff that keeps the cars and trucks and buses running? It comes from *oil*, which comes from the rocks.

But how did oil get into rocks?

Oil, like coal, is something that was once alive. That's why it gives us heat. Oil is what is left of plants and animals that died millions of years ago in quiet parts of the sea. Some of the plants were seaweeds. Some were algae, the tiny plants that make a green scum on top of standing water. What the animals were we don't know.

Well, they died and turned to fatty oil. And mud covered them. And sand covered the mud. And by and by there were shale and sandstone and dark, fatty oil. And then, luckily for us, the oil began to move. For if it hadn't, we never would have been able to get it out.

Men drill through rock to pools of oil below.

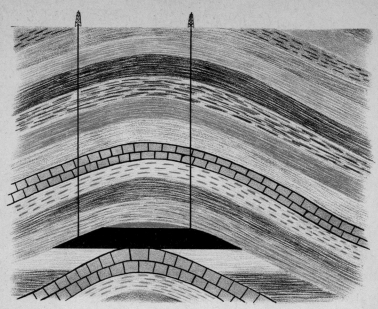

Salt water from an early sea lies beneath the oil.

We can't pump oil out so long as it's *in* the rock.

The oil moved very slowly. It moved through pores in the rocks till it found an empty place. And there it settled in pools—some large, some small. These are what men try to find when they drill down through the rocks. It is such pools we mean when we say somebody "struck oil."

Think how many cars and trucks and buses there are! Are they all running around on seaweeds and algae? Could there have been that many seaweeds and algae in all the world?

We have to believe there were. And it's really not so hard to do. For millions of years is a long time. Millions of years made thick beds of coal. Millions of years made thick beds of chalk. Millions of years could make deep pools of oil.

Besides, the proof is down there. It is right under the pools. There is water under the oil, and it can't be rain. Whatever made the oil *must* have lived in the sea. For this is salt water. It is some of the sea of millions of years ago. It is some of the sea that was trapped in the mud that now has turned to shale.

13. Every Rock Has a Story to Tell

You have heard people say, "There's nothing new under the sun." In a way it is true. For nature keeps doing the same things over and over again.

Take rain, for example. Rain turns into a brook. The brook becomes a river. The river flows into the sea. The sun heats the water and it turns to vapor. The vapor becomes clouds. And rain falls again. Rain, brook, river, sea, vapor, clouds, rain. Over and over again.

But does this mean there is nothing new under the sun? No. It only means there is no waste. A patchwork quilt is made of left-over pieces, but it's a new quilt just the same. Sedimentary rock is made out of bits of other rocks, but it is new.

It would be far truer to say, "There is always something new under the sun." For the earth is always changing. From minute to minute it is never the same. Here a rock has cracked. Here a pebble has lost a chip. Here a chip has been ground to sand. And here new rock has been made.

The clay for pottery comes from rock.

Not so long ago people thought the rocks were finished. They thought rocks had been made once for all. But we see now that rocks are still being made. Every day. All the time.

New rock comes pouring out from the hot depths of the earth. Sediment is being laid down by the waves. It will make patchwork rock. Shells are piling up on the floor of the sea. Some day those shells will be limestone. Granite is somewhere turning into gneiss. Shale is somewhere turning to slate. Peat is somewhere turning to coal. Every minute there's something new in the world. A wonderful play is going on. And he who has eyes to see can watch it.

Back in the beginning of this book we said, "Every rock in the world has had adventures." Now you know it's true. It is true of sandstone and basalt and marble. It is true of boulders and pebbles and sand. Whatever *is* rock or *has been* rock has a story to tell. That story is a tiny part in the great play that goes on all the time.

There's the teapot on your table. It was

Scouring powder may contain pumice, a rock foam.

The soil in this pot came from rock.

feldspar once. For clay is crumbled feldspar.
Maybe that feldspar came from giant granite.
Then think what a journey it took from the
hot depths of the earth! How long did it lie
cooling in the dark? How long before it saw
the light of day?

Sprinkle a little salt into your hand. Does it bring you a picture of America ages ago? The sea that covered the land is rolling away. One arm only has been left behind. The climate is hot and dry. The water in the cut-off arm gets lower and lower. At last only the salt is left.

Scour the sink with powder. Do you see the lava flowing? Here at the edge of the flow is foam. It will be pumice when it hardens.

A plant stands on the window sill. How many millions of years did nature take to make that soil? Do you see the lichens on the rock?

The window pane was sandstone once. Can you see the waves lift up the sediment and carry it out to sea?

Go outdoors. Maybe the sun is shining. Maybe the rain is falling. Maybe the wind is blowing. Whatever the weather is doing, you can be sure it is doing something to the rocks. It is breaking and building, breaking and building.

Take a stone in your hand. Now that you understand, try to read its story.

Index

Marble, 61
Mica, 40-41
Moon, 12
Mountains, 9, 12-14, 53

Oil, 69-72

Pacific Ocean, 12
Patchwork rocks, 19-21
Peat, 67
Pebbles, 16, 23
Plants, 26, 62-66, 69
Plaster of Paris, 49
Pumice, 36-37, 78

Quartz, 40
Quartzite, 60

Rain, 10, 45-46, 73

Salt, 45-47, 78
Sand, 18

Sandstone, 22, 60
Sea, 17, 46-49, 53, 72
Sea water, 52
Seaweeds, 69
Sediment, 17, 19-20
Sedimentary rock,
    21, 74
Shale, 23, 60, 72
Shell limestone, 54, 61
Shells, 53-56
Slate, 60
Soil, 6, 25-29
Streams, 16-17

Topsoil, 28

Volcanoes, 31-37

Water, 46, 52
Waves, 17, 20
White Cliffs of
    Dover, 55